W9-DFF-420

Erin Pembrey Swan

Pelicans, Cormorants, and Their Kin

Franklin Watts - A Division of Scholastic Inc.
New York • Toronto • London • Auckland • Sydney
Mexico City • New Delhi • Hong Kong
Danbury, Connecticut

For Sara, because of everything she has done for me.

Photographs © 2002: BBC Natural History Unit: 5 top right, 23 (Jeff Foott), 8, 25, 31 (Pete Oxford), 33 (Peter Reese), 41 (Warwick Sloss), 5 top left (John Sparks), cover, 6 (Lynn Stone); Dembinsky Photo Assoc.: 39 (Barbara Gerlach), 17 (Mark J. Thomas); Minden Pictures: 9 (Jim Brandenburg), 43 (Tui De Roy), 1, 19 (Tim Fitzharris), 5 bottom right (Konrad Wothe); Peter Arnold Inc./Kelvin Aitken: 29; Photo Researchers, NY: 27 (Edmund Appel), 21 (Marshall Sklar), 37 (Sandy Sprunt); VIREO/Academy of Natural Sciences of Philadelphia/R.L. Pitman: 35; Visuals Unlimited: 14, 15 (Hal Beral), 5 bottom left (Jakub Jasinski), 42 (Bill Kamin), 7 (Arthur Morris).

Illustrations by Pedro Julio Gonzalez, Steve Savage, and A. Natacha Pimentel C.

The photo on the cover shows a brown pelican with a fish in its mouth. The photo on the title page shows a flock of white pelicans.

Library of Congress Cataloging-in-Publication Data

Swan, Erin Pembrey.
 Pelicans, cormorants, and their kin / Erin Pembrey Swan; [Pedro Julio Gonzalez, Steve Savage, and A. Natacha Pimentel C., illustrators].
   p. cm. – (An animals in order book)
 Includes bibliographical references and index.
 Summary: Examines pelicans, cormorants, and related birds and describes their relationship with people.
  ISBN 0-531-11929-7 (lib. bdg.)   0-531-16378-4 (pbk.)
  1. Pelicans—Juvenile literature. 2. Cormorants—Juvenile literature. [1. Pelicans. 2. Cormorants.] I. Gonzalez, Pedro Julio, ill. II. Savage, Steve, ill. III. Pimentel C., A. Natacha, ill. IV. Title. V. Animals in order.
QL696.P47 S82 2002
598.4'3—dc21   2001005730

Contents

Meet the Pelicans, Cormorants, and Their Kin

Have you ever seen a pelican with a bill full of fish? Did you notice the special pouch attached to the pelican's bill and wonder if the bird uses it for anything other than catching fishes? If so, what would that be? And what other birds are similar to pelicans? Which ones are their close relatives?

Pelicans belong to the order *pelecaniformes*. There are six families in this order, which in turn are made up of many different kinds of birds. Some of them are similar to pelicans, while others seem very different. However, all of these birds have a few important things in common. These similarities make these birds members of the order pelecaniformes.

Three of the birds on the next page are pelecaniformes. One of them is not. Can you guess which bird is not a pelecaniforme?

Red-footed booby

White-tailed tropic bird

White stork

Dalmation pelican

Traits of the Pelecaniformes

Did you guess the white stork? You were right! How could you tell that the stork is not a pelecaniforme?

If you look at the stork's feet, you will notice that its toes are separate from each other. All pelecaniformes, however, have webbed feet. This means that their toes are connected to each other by thin *membranes* of skin. The webs on their feet help the pelecaniformes swim quickly so they can catch their meals. All pelecaniformes eat fishes and other animals that live in water, such as squids, prawns, and frogs. Many of them dive underwater and chase their food until they catch it. They need to be fast swimmers so they can eat.

Pelecaniformes have webbed feet that help them swim.

A pelican uses its gular sac to catch fish.

Almost all pelicaniformes have throat pouches, which are called *gular sacs*. Pelicans have the largest gular sacs of all the pelecaniformes. They use them most often to scoop fish out of the water, like a fisherman uses a net. Other pelecaniformes have smaller gular sacs. They use them in many different ways. Some pelecaniformes, such as frigate

This frigate bird is inflating his gular sac to attract a mate.

birds, puff up their gular sacs in order to attract mates. Others, such as cormorants, use their pouches to give them the extra space they need for positioning fish properly before they swallow them whole. Most pelecaniformes also use their gular sacs to cool down. In hot weather, they flutter them in and out. This action cools them off just as panting cools off a dog and sweating cools off a human.

Another important trait that is common to the pelecaniformes is their skeletons. All birds have a special bone called a *furcula*. The furcula is a flexible, V-shaped bone that attaches birds' wings to their bodies. It helps move birds' wings up and down when they fly. In the pelecaniformes, the furcula is attached more securely to the breastbone than it is in other birds. This helps them keep their wings steady so they can glide easily in the air. Thanks to their furcula design, some pelecaniformes can hover in the air for a long time without using much energy. This is important for birds that catch fish in the water. Sometimes they have to hang in the air for quite a while until they spot food in the water below. Then they glide down quickly and snatch their *prey* before it can escape.

Most pelecaniformes are also very social birds. They often live together in large *colonies* near the ocean or other bodies of water. Like all birds, pelecaniformes lay eggs that hatch into chicks. Pelecaniformes are born naked and defenseless. Their parents feed them partly digested fish and other sea creatures straight from their bills. Most pelecaniformes live long lives. It is common for a pelicaniforme to live for up to twenty years.

Pelecaniformes often live in large colonies.

The Order of Living Things

A tiger has more in common with a house cat than with a daisy. A true bug is more like a butterfly than a jellyfish. Scientists arrange living things into groups based on how they look and how they act. A tiger and a house cat belong to the same group, but a daisy belongs to a different group.

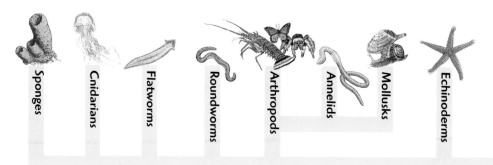

Sponges Cnidarians Flatworms Roundworms Arthropods Annelids Mollusks Echinoderms

Animals

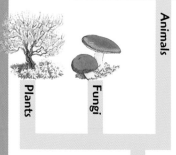

Plants Fungi

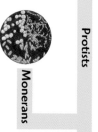

Protists

Monerans

All living things can be placed in one of five groups called *kingdoms*: the plant kingdom, the animal kingdom, the fungus kingdom, the moneran kingdom, or the protist kingdom. You can probably name many of the creatures in the plant and animal kingdoms. The fungus kingdom includes mushrooms, yeasts, and molds. The moneran and protist kingdoms contain thousands of living things that are too small to see without a microscope.

10

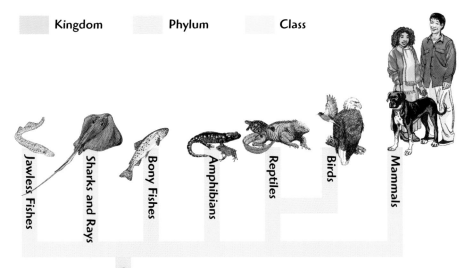

Kingdom   Phylum   Class

Jawless Fishes

Sharks and Rays

Bony Fishes

Amphibians

Reptiles

Birds

Mammals

Chordates

Because there are millions and millions of living things on Earth, some of the members of one kingdom may not seem all that similar. The animal kingdom includes creatures as different as tarantulas and trout, jellyfish and jaguars, salamanders and sparrows, elephants and earthworms.

To show that an elephant is more like a jaguar than an earthworm, scientists further separate the creatures in each kingdom into more specific groups. The animal kingdom can be divided into nine *phyla*. Humans belong to the chordate phylum. Almost all chordates have a backbone.

Each phylum can be subdivided into many *classes*. Humans, mice, and elephants all belong to the mammal class. Each class can be further divided into orders; orders into *families*, families into *genera*, and genera into *species*. All the members of a species are very similar.

How the Pelecaniformes Fit In

You probably can guess that members of the order pelecaniformes belong to the animal kingdom. They have much more in common with spiders and snakes than they do with maple trees and morning glories.

Pelecaniformes are members of the chordate phylum. All chordates have backbones and skeletons. Can you think of some other chordates? Examples include elephants, mice, snakes, frogs, fishes, whales, and humans. All birds belong to the same class. There are about thirty orders of birds. Pelecaniformes makes up one of these orders.

Scientists divide pelecaniformes into six families and several genera. There are fifty-seven species of pelecaniformes. They live near oceans and freshwater lakes throughout the world. In this book you will learn more about fourteen species of pelecaniformes.

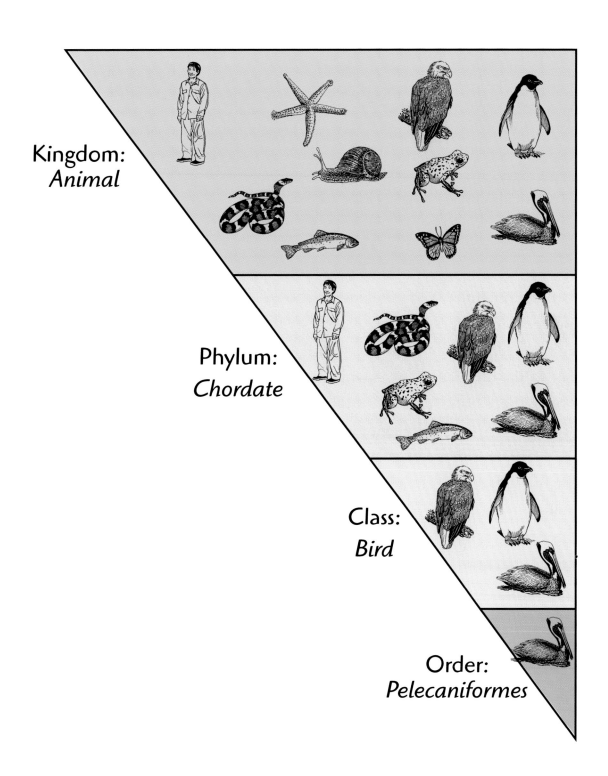

Kingdom:
Animal

Phylum:
Chordate

Class:
Bird

Order:
Pelecaniformes

Pelicans

FAMILY: Pelecanidae
COMMON EXAMPLE: Brown pelican
GENUS AND SPECIES: *Pelecanus occidentalis*
SIZE: 48 inches (114 centimeters)

A brown pelican cruises over the ocean, searching for fishes in the water below. It spots a school of menhaden and quickly plunges into the water after the fleeing fish. Using the large gular sac under its bill as a net, the pelican scoops up mouthfuls of menhaden and seawater. Then it bobs back up to the surface and lets the water drain out of its bill before gulping down its tasty catch.

A pelican can use its gular sac to capture pounds of the fish it loves to eat. A brown pelican's gular sac can hold up to 3 gallons (0.8 liters) of fish and water. That's three times as much as its stomach can hold! That's why the pelican must drain all the water in its sac before swallowing. Menhaden is a brown pelican's favorite fish, but it will also eat pigfish, pinfish, herring, mullet, and prawns.

Brown pelicans live in large, friendly groups on the Pacific, Atlantic, and Gulf coasts as far north as Nova Scotia. They build reed-and-twig nests in trees or in shallow scrapes in the ground, where the females hatch two or three chalky-white eggs at a time. After the young pelicans hatch, it takes about one year before they are strong enough to glide through the air as well as their parents can. Then special air sacs under their skin and in their bones help them stay high up in the sky. If they spot fish in the water, though, these young pelicans quickly go plunging headfirst into the ocean after their lunch.

Boobies

FAMILY: Sulidae
COMMON EXAMPLE: Blue-footed booby
GENUS AND SPECIES: *Sula nebouxii*
SIZE: 32 to 34 inches (81 to 86 cm)

A male blue-footed booby has spotted a female he likes. He tilts his beak, tail, and wings to the sky, letting out a high-pitched whistle that is sure to catch her attention. Some scientists call this skypointing. While she hides her bill shyly in her feathers, he "dances" around her slowly, showing off his bright blue feet. Sometimes the male even offers her a piece of nesting material such as a twig, the way a human would offer a bouquet of flowers. If she likes him too, she skypoints back. After they mate, the female lays two or three eggs that she keeps warm with her large, webbed feet.

Blue-footed boobies dwell mostly on the Galapagos Islands, a cluster of dry islands off the northern coast of South American. They can also be found as far north as California. Their name, "booby," comes from the Spanish word *bobo*, which means "clown" or "stupid fellow." They got this name because they landed on the Spanish explorers' ships and were easily caught and killed by the sailors.

Large groups of blue-footed boobies live and hunt together along the coasts. They glide over the ocean in flocks, looking for anchovies and other fish in the water below. Once they spot them, they dive straight down from heights of up to 80 feet (25 meters)! They fold

16

their wings back at the last minute and plunge into the water after
the fish. One by one, each booby follows another in perfectly timed
movements, until almost all of them have had something to eat.

Cormorants

FAMILY: Phalacrocoracidae

COMMON EXAMPLE: Double-crested
    cormorant

GENUS AND SPECIES: *Phalacrocorax auritus*

SIZE: 33 inches (84 cm)

A double-crested cormorant dips underwater after a fish. It kicks with its feet to propel it through the water, using its wings to brake. With one quick dart of its hooked bill, it snags the unlucky fish and glides back to the surface to gulp it down. When the cormorant has had its fill of fish, it sits on the shore with its wings outspread, drying them in the sun.

If the cormorant has babies, however, it flies back to its seaweed-lined nest to its two or three hungry chicks. The cormorant coughs the half-digested fish back up into its mouth and the chicks peck it straight out of its beak. Young double-crested cormorants have huge appetites. They eat about six times a day if there is enough food to go around. When they are about one month old, the young birds begin to explore the world outside the nest. A few weeks later, they start learning how to fly.

Double-crested cormorants live in small groups along the Atlantic and Pacific coasts of North America. They also dwell further inland, where they hunt in freshwater lakes for their food. Although they like fish best, they also eat crayfishes and frogs if they find them. Two

18

curly, black crests mark the heads of double-crested cormorants. They lose these crests in winter, however, usually after mating. After the female lays her eggs, both parents take turns keeping them warm with their webbed feet. When the chicks hatch, both parents have a busy job keeping the bellies of their hungry chicks filled with fish.

Cormorants

FAMILY: Phalacrocoracidae
COMMON EXAMPLE: Red-legged cormorant
GENUS AND SPECIES: *Phalacrocorax gaimardi*
SIZE: 30 inches (75 cm)

A female red-legged cormorant flies back to her nest to take her turn keeping her eggs warm. Her mate has been *incubating* the eggs long enough to get hungry. He stands up and makes room for her on the nest. Then he stretches his wings and glides off in search of some tasty fish to catch and eat. The female fluffs her feathers and settles down over the eggs. The eggs will hatch about a month after they are laid. Then both parents will have a busy job keeping their three or four hungry chicks well fed with fish, squid, and other ocean treats.

Red-legged cormorants get their name from (you guessed it) their bright red legs and feet. Unlike double-crested cormorants, they live only on the coasts, close to the ocean homes of the fish and squid they like to eat. Red-legged cormorants can be found along the South American coasts, all the way from Peru to the most southern tip of the continent. They usually nest alone, but sometimes gather in small groups. Red-legged cormorants often mix their nests among colonies of boobies and other cormorant species, where they seem to feel most at home.

Similar to double-crested cormorants, red-legged cormorants dive underwater to catch their meals. They either plunge from the air or

dip under the water while swimming on the surface. They trap fish in their sharp beaks and rise to the surface before swallowing them. Their small gular sacs and flexible necks help them position fishes perfectly so they can swallow them whole and headfirst.

Anhingas

FAMILY: Anhingidae
COMMON EXAMPLE: Anhinga
GENUS AND SPECIES: *Anhinga anhinga*
SIZE: 34 to 36 inches (86 to 91 cm)

An anhinga cruises through the water with its head and neck showing above the surface. With only its slender head poking up, it looks like a swimming snake. That is why it is also known as a snakebird. When the anhinga spots a fish, it darts its S-shaped neck forward and spears the fish with its razor-sharp bill. With one quick movement, it flips the fish in the air and catches it in its mouth. Yum! Another tasty fish is swallowed whole.

Anhingas do not produce oil to keep their feathers dry underwater. They can swim faster if their feathers are completely wet. After diving for fish, however, they must sit in the sun with their wings stretched out to dry. If they didn't do this, it would be hard for them to fly with heavy, wet feathers.

Swampy lakes and rivers surrounded by plenty of trees are the anhinga's favorite places to live. It likes warm regions in which it is easy to dry its feathers after swimming. Anhingas are found throughout the tropics of the Caribbean and the Americas, but have been spotted as far north as New York. They prefer to live alone, but sometimes build their nests close to colonies of double-crested cormorants or herons. Once their nests are built and their chicks have

hatched, anhingas will do anything to protect their babies. They usually just snap their beaks at intruders to scare them off, but if they have to, anhingas will fight with their wings and sharp bills until they drive the enemy away.

Boobies

FAMILY: Sulidae
COMMON EXAMPLE: Peruvian booby
GENUS AND SPECIES: *Sula variegata*
SIZE: 32 inches (81 cm)

Peruvian boobies do not have to look far for food, since they live near one of the richest fishing areas in the world. The Humboldt upwelling of cold, *nutrient*-rich water off the coast of Peru and northern Chile provides food for millions of anchovies and other fish. It is a perfect place for the anchovy-loving Peruvian booby to live. Unlike other boobies, these lucky birds often raise as many as four chicks at a time because there is plenty of food to go around. Once these chicks are about three or four years old, they are ready to hatch babies of their own.

When Peruvian boobies are old enough to hatch chicks, they begin looking around for mates. If two Peruvian boobies like each other, they parade around, lift their heads high, and may even fence with their bills. Then they settle down to the serious task of building a nest. They gather twigs, dirt, and anything else they can find that will make a good nest. Once the eggs are laid, both parents take turns keeping them warm until they hatch. Their large webbed feet help keep the eggs cozy and safe.

Like blue-footed boobies, Peruvian boobies are masters at catching fish. They dive like missiles from amazing heights and plummet

24

into the water after their meals. Since their eyes are close to the fronts of their heads, Peruvian boobies have no trouble spotting fish in the water below, even from 50 feet (16 m) up!

Pelicans

FAMILY: Pelecanidae
COMMON EXAMPLE: Dalmation Pelican
GENUS AND SPECIES: *Pelecanus crispus*
SIZE: 67 inches (170 cm)

A flock of Dalmation pelicans flies single-file over the sparkling blue water of the Mediterranean Sea. The birds are heading toward their winter nesting grounds in Egypt. After a long summer spent in Eastern Europe, these pelicans want to avoid the region's harsh winter. They would rather warm themselves along the sunny banks of the Nile, where there is plenty of fish to go around.

Dalmation pelicans have a special trick for catching fish. They gather in a group near a school of fish and then "herd" them toward shallow water. When the fish are stuck in the shallow water, the pelicans have an easy time scooping them up in their gular sacs and swallowing them whole.

Sometimes a Dalmation pelican just sits on the surface and dips its bill into the water when it spots a fish. It nets the unlucky fish with its sac, drains the water, and swallows another meal.

Dalmation pelicans range from Eastern Europe to Central Asia in the summer months. When winter comes, however, they fly as far south as Egypt and northern India.

They build their nests and hatch their chicks in swamps or near shallow lakes. The males gather grass and twigs for the females, who

weave cozy nests that rest on mats of floating vegetation. After they hatch, the noisy chicks wait eagerly for their parents to bring them food. They stick their heads deep into their parents' throats to grab half-digested fishes with their tiny bills. They are able to hunt for themselves fairly quickly, but they cannot hatch their own chicks until they are at least three years old.

Darters

FAMILY: Anhingidae
COMMON EXAMPLE: Asian darter
GENUS AND SPECIES: *Anhinga melanogaster*
SIZE: 34 to 36 inches (86 to 91 cm)

An Asian darter stretches its wings in a patch of sun on a warm riverbank. After swimming underwater to catch a fish, the darter's feathers are soaked through. Since it does not have oil glands to keep its feathers waterproof, the darter has to dry its wings in the sun before it can fly again. Once they are dry, however, the darter soars easily through the sky, gliding from one air current to the next.

Similar to their close relatives, the anhingas, Asian darters hunt underwater for their meals. They swim with only their narrow heads poking above the surface. When they spot some fishes, they dip underwater and spear them with their knifelike bills. A special hinge in their necks allows them to dart their bills forward quickly, catching the fish before they escape. Darters also have jagged edges on their bills that hold fish tightly so they cannot get away. When they are not hunting fish, Asian darters snap up insects from the surface of the water.

Asian darters make their homes near water in the warm, temperate regions of Asia, Africa, and Australia. When male darters are ready to breed, they choose nest sites and decorate them with fresh green leaves. They attract females by waving their wings and shaking

nearby twigs with their bills. If a female likes a male and the nest site he has chosen, she helps build a nest with the twigs and grass that he collects, usually in the fork of a tree. The eggs hatch about a month after they are laid, and then the parents have a busy time keeping their noisy chicks well fed with half-digested fish.

Cormorants

FAMILY: Phalacrocoracidae
COMMON EXAMPLE: Flightless cormorant
GENUS AND SPECIES: *Phalacrocorax harrisi*
SIZE: 35 to 39 inches (89 to 100 cm)

This cormorant may not be able to fly, but it certainly can swim. A flightless cormorant glides through the water, propelling itself with powerful kicks. Extra webbing on its feet helps it swim faster than other cormorants. This makes it easier for it to catch the tiny squid fleeing in front of it. The cormorant kicks once more, darts it head forward, and snatches a squid in its beak. Success! The cormorant swims back to shore, hops out of the water, and scrambles over the rocks to share its catch with its chicks.

Flightless cormorants are one of the few bird species that cannot fly. Their *ancestors* have always lived on the Galapagos Islands, where they had few enemies. They were so safe that, over time, they lost the ability to fly. Flightless cormorants have only stubby wings that are too small for flying. They have to rely on swimming to catch their meals. Flightless cormorants feed no more than 330 feet (100 m) offshore, feasting on treats such as squid, octopuses, eels, and various kinds of fish.

Even though they cannot use their wings to fly, flightless cormorants still dry them after swimming. It is a funny sight to see one stretching out its stumpy wings to dry in the sun. Once its wings are

dry, the cormorant waddles back to its nest to feed its chicks. Flight-less cormorants can *breed* up to three times a year, which helps keep their population large.

Shags

FAMILY: Phalacrocoracidae
COMMON EXAMPLE: Spotted shag
GENUS AND SPECIES: *Phalacrocorax punctatus*
SIZE: 25 to 31 inches (65 to 80 cm)

The cliffs along the New Zealand coast are quite noisy with young spotted shags waiting to be fed. The chicks chirp and squawk loudly from nests built on narrow ledges along the cliffs. Although they are born naked and defenseless, the chicks are kept safe by the large colony of shags in which they live. The hungry birds scan the skies for their parents, hoping they will return quickly with a delicious mouthful of sardines or mullet.

Spotted shags are a type of cormorant. They sometimes will nest near other types of cormorants for safety. They have long, sharp bills that are perfect for snagging fish in the ocean, and small, blue gular sacs. Shags push their sacs in and out to stay cool, flash them to signal other shags, and use them as extra space when they position fish for swallowing them whole.

Shags are designed for efficient swimming and flying. Their legs are placed far back on their bodies, which makes it difficult for them to walk. Although they waddle awkwardly on land, shags are agile swimmers and flyers. They fly low over the ocean, scanning the depths for mullet and sardines. When they spot some, they dive into the water and begin the chase. They press their wings tightly to their

bodies, stretch their necks forward, and kick with their strong, webbed feet. With a single dart of their heads, they snatch the fish and kick toward the surface to drain excess seawater from their gular sacs before swallowing them. After they have eaten, the shags stretch out their wings to dry and bask in the warm sun of the South Pacific.

Tropic birds

FAMILY: Phaethontidae
COMMON EXAMPLE: Red-tailed tropic bird
GENUS AND SPECIES: *Phaethon rubricauda*
SIZE: 19 inches (47 cm), 37 inches (94 cm)
with tail feathers

Nested cozily inside a crevice in an island cliff, a baby red-tailed tropic bird peeps with excitement when it sees its parents returning with food. They have been gone for a whole day, searching the ocean for fish to feed themselves and their baby. The mother lands in the nest and coughs up half-digested squid for her hungry baby. Fed with a diet of squid and small fish, the young tropic bird grows quickly. When it is only about three months old, it is ready for life on its own. Then it flies out over the ocean in search of food. After about three or four years by itself, the young tropic bird will return to the colony ready to have its own babies.

Adult red-tailed tropic birds are known for their bright red beaks and long, red tail feathers that stream out behind them as they fly. Young tropic birds are born with black beaks and no tail feathers, but that changes as they mature. A tropic bird's tail feathers become redder during breeding season, when large groups of tropic birds swoop and squawk through the air in search of mates. Once a pair has mated, the female lays a single red-brown egg in a cliff hole or on bare ground under a boulder or bush.

Red-tailed tropic birds live on islands and along coasts in the tropical Pacific and Indian Oceans. Since their short legs are placed so far back on their bodies, it is very hard for them to walk on land. Except during breeding season, they spend all their time at sea. They cruise over the ocean, scanning the water for food. If they spot a tasty fish or squid, they plunge after it and catch it in their sharp beaks. Then they glide back into the air, their long tail feathers streaming behind them.

Tropic birds

FAMILY: Phaethontidae
COMMON EXAMPLE: White-tailed tropic bird
GENUS AND SPECIES: *Phaethon lepturus*
SIZE: 18 inches (45 cm)

High above the warm waters of the Indian Ocean, a white-tailed tropic bird hovers almost motionless in the sky. With its long tail feathers trailing behind it and its graceful wings flapping gently, the tropic bird searches the ocean for fish to catch. If it sees a flying fish, its favorite food, it swoops down and grabs the fish in midleap. Although tropic birds like flying fish the best, they will also eat squid, crabs, and even snails. Sometimes they dive into the water to snag their prey.

Since tropic birds have very short legs, it is almost impossible for them to walk on land. They spend most of their time in the air, where they feel most comfortable. Tropic birds even court each other in midair. The graceful birds swoop around in groups, males and females squawking loudly at each other. If a male and female like each other, they land at a nest site and squawk at each other some more before they mate.

White-tailed tropic birds live together in large colonies through-out the tropics. They nest on islands in the Atlantic, Pacific, and Indian Oceans, wherever it is warm and sunny. Tropic birds build their nests on cliff ledges and sometimes in trees, where the female

lays a single egg. The newly hatched, downy chick grows quickly.
After about three months, it is ready for its first flight lesson. Soon it
will be swooping and gliding with its parents.

Frigate birds

FAMILY: Fregatidae
COMMON EXAMPLE: Great frigate bird
GENUS AND SPECIES: *Fregata minor*
SIZE: 39 inches (100 cm)

Two half-grown great frigate birds swoop and dive together through the air. One of them carries a stick in its bill, which the other bird keeps trying to steal. It pesters its friend by darting toward it again and again. When its friend drops the stick, the other one snags it before it hits the water. These two youngsters are playing a game that helps them practice for when they are full-grown and must hunt for their own food.

Some people call frigate birds pirates because of how they fetch their meals. Since they do not have any oil glands to keep their feathers dry, frigate birds cannot dive into the ocean to catch their own fish. Instead, they hover in the air, waiting for some other bird to appear with a bill full of fish. Then they glide forward and harass the bird until it drops its catch. Sometimes they snatch it out of the air, but usually they grab the fish from the water's surface. Frigate birds also grab flying fish in midleap and pick up dead fish off the surface of the water.

Great frigate birds nest in colonies on islands throughout the Pacific, Atlantic, and Indian Oceans. During breeding season, males attract females by puffing up their gular sacs into bright red balloons.

After they pair up, each couple builds its nest, usually in low shrubs along the shore. Then each female lays a single egg. When the chick hatches, it grows slowly. It cannot hatch its own chicks until it is about seven years old. Since they mature so slowly, frigate birds live for a long time. Some of them live as long as twenty-five years, which is old for a bird!

Gannets

FAMILY: Sulidae
COMMON EXAMPLE: Northern gannet
GENUS AND SPECIES: *Morus bassanus*
SIZE: 31 inches (80 cm)

It is autumn along the coast of Great Britain and flocks of northern gannets are getting ready to fly south for the winter. These gannets will fly as far south as West Africa to escape the chilly winter winds. When it is spring, they will return north to their favorite nesting grounds on Britain's cliffs and islands.

Northern gannets live together in crowded colonies throughout the North Atlantic, from Canada and the United States to Europe. Males and females court each other by standing face to face with their wings outspread before knocking their bills together and bowing. Then they gather seaweed and driftwood to build their nests. Sometimes they make their nests so close together that the chicks in each nest can reach out and touch each other.

A colony of northern gannets can be pretty loud. While the adults call to each other with harsh cries, the chicks peep loudly to their parents, as if to say "feed me." When the adults fly out to sea, however, they make no noise at all.

Fish such as mackerel and herring are a northern gannet's favorite food, but it will also eat cod, menhaden, sand lance, and squid. Gannets usually hunt by diving into the water after their prey,

sometimes from as high up in the air as 150 feet (45 m)! Although sometimes they hunt alone, gannets usually flock together to catch their food. They cruise in groups over the ocean in search of fish, their strong wings keeping them high up in the air. Northern gannets are among the largest seabirds in the north Atlantic, so when they dive into the ocean after their prey, they make quite a splash!

Pelecaniformes and People

Pelecaniformes can be very useful to people. In Asia, people use cormorants to help them catch fish. Fishermen tie collars around the cormorants' necks to keep them from swallowing the fish. Then the fishermen attach long lines to the cormorants' legs and let them out to dive after a meal. When the cormorants catch fish, the fishermen haul the birds back to the boat and take the fish out of their bills. Only a few fishermen still practice this tradition, since it is easier to catch fish in nets.

There are other ways in which people affect the pelecaniformes. Sometimes pelecaniformes and people hunt the same fish. Peruvian boobies in the Pacific Ocean feed mostly on anchovies. People also like to eat anchovies, however. Some fisherman have caught so many of

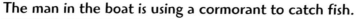

The man in the boat is using a cormorant to catch fish.

these fish that there are very few left for the Peruvian boobies to eat. Because of this food shortage, there are fewer Peruvian boobies alive today.

Pelecaniforme populations have also decreased because of the human use of toxic chemicals. In the late 1940s farmers started using a chemical called DDT to kill insects that ate their crops. When DDT washed off the crops and ran into the water, it *contaminated* the fish that the pelecaniformes hunted. When the birds ate the fish, they became contaminated as well. When they laid eggs, the eggshells were so thin that they broke before the chicks could hatch. Many pelecaniforme chicks died this way, which dramatically reduced the populations of birds such as cormorants. Since then, however, the use of DDT has been banned and the pelican population is increasing.

Pelecaniformes, like this brown pelican, are threatened by some things that humans do.

Pelecaniformes are also in danger because people have taken over much of their *habitat*. There are fewer pelicans alive today than there used to be because so much of their natural habitat has been destroyed to make room for people, their houses, and their garbage.

What can be done to help endangered pelecaniformes? The use of DDT was stopped altogether by 1990. Some pelecaniformes are now protected on wildlife preserves. Can you think of more ways to help pelecaniformes survive?

Words to Know

ancestors—a member of a plant or animal family that came before

breed—to mate and produce young

class—a group of creatures within a phylum that shares certain characteristics

colony—a large group of animals, such as birds, that live and nest together

contaminate—to soil, stain, or infect

family—a group of creatures within an order that shares certain characteristics

furcula—a V-shaped flexible bone that attaches a bird's wings to its breastbone

genus (plural genera)—a group of creatures within an order that shares certain characteristics

gular sac—a loose pouch attached to the bills of some birds

habitat—the natural environment of an animal or plant

hover—to remain suspended above a place or object

incubate—to keep warm until an egg hatches

kingdom—one of the five categories into which all living things are placed: the animal kingdom, the plant kingdom, the fungus kingdom, the moneran kingdom, and the protist kingdom

membrane—a thin, soft, flexible sheet or layer of skin

nutrient—a substance that promotes growth and health

order—a group of creatures within a class that shares certain characteristisc

phylum (plural phyla)—a group of creatures within a kingdom that shares certain characteristics

prey—an animal that is hunted by another for food

species—a group of creatures within a genus that shares the certain characteristics

Learning More

Books

Harrison, Peter. *Seabirds of the World*. Princeton, NJ: Princeton University Press, 1996.

Perkins, Simon. *Familiar Birds of Sea and Shore (National Audubon Society Pocket Guides)*. New York: Knopf, 1994.

Tesar, Jenny E. *What on Earth Is a Booby? (What on Earth Series)*. Woodbridge, CT: Blackbirch Press, 1997.

Video

Audubon Society's VideoGuide to Birds of North America. Vol. 1

Web Sites

Cornell Laboratory of Ornithology
http://www.ornith.cornell.edu
This site features a bird of the week, bird projects, and information about how people can help protect the world's birds.

Pelican Man's Bird Sanctuary
http://www.pelicanman.org/
This site contains information on a pelican sanctuary in Sarasota, Florida, where injured pelicans are rehabilitated.

Peterson Online
http://www.Petersononline.com/birds/
This site has pictures of rare birds, links to birding sites, virtual tours, and tips on how to find birds in your area.

Index

About the Author

Erin Pembrey Swan studied animal behavior, literature, and early childhood education at Hampshire College in Massachusetts. She also studied literature and history at University College Galway in Ireland and creative writing at New School University in Manhattan. Her poetry has been published in various journals, both in the United States and in Ireland. Ms. Swan has written six other books in the Animals in Order series, including *Primates: From Howlers Monkeys to Humans*, *Land Predators of North America*, and *Kangaroos and Koalas: What They Have in Common*. She is also the author of *India*, a book in the Enchantment of the World series. Ms. Swan currently lives and works in New York City.

SUGAR GROVE PUBLIC LIBRARY DISTRICT
54 Snow Street/P.O. Box 1049
Sugar Grove, IL 60554
(630) 466-4686